first book of
dogs

Isabel Thomas

A & C BLACK
AN IMPRINT OF BLOOMSBURY
LONDON   NEW DELHI   NEW YORK   SYDNEY

Published 2014 by
A&C Black
An imprint of Bloomsbury Publishing Plc
50 Bedford Square, London, WC1B 3DP

www.bloomsbury.com

ISBN 978-1-4729-0397-6

This book is produced using paper that is made from wood
grown in managed, sustainable forests. It is natural, renewable
and recyclable. The logging and manufacturing processes
conform to the environmental regulations of the country of origin.

Printed in China by Leo Paper Products, Heshan, Guangdong

10 9 8 7 6 5 4 3 2 1

Dog safety

Always have an adult with you when you look at dogs.
Ask the owner's permission before patting or stroking
a dog. Be quiet and gentle when you are near dogs.

Contents

Dogs

Dogs are amazing animals. Look out for guard dogs, police dogs, farm dogs, and guide dogs hard at work. Listen out for pet dogs barking and having fun on walks.

You can spot dogs in towns and cities, in the countryside, and at dog shows. This book will help you to name the different breeds you see. It tells you about their colours and patterns, and shows you some special features.

At the back of this book is a Spotter's Guide to help you remember the dogs you spot. Tick the breeds off as you see them. You can also find out about the different groups of dogs here.

Turn the page to find out all about dogs!

Afghan Hound

Afghan Hounds look like pampered princesses. They are actually hard-working hunters and watchdogs. When it's time to relax, Afghan Hounds love to play.

The first Afghan Hounds came from Afghanistan.

Long head

Ears covered in long fur

Long, silky coat

Long legs

Their long coats need brushing or combing every day.

Feet covered with fur

Basset Hound

Woof! If you hear a booming bark, it might be a Basset Hound. These loud dogs are actually calm and friendly. They like to take it easy and are often caught napping.

> A Basset Hound's long ears can get very dirty on walks.

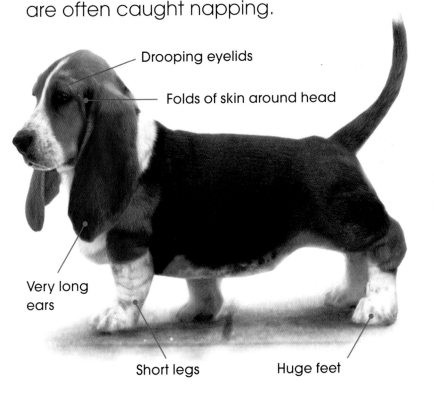

Drooping eyelids

Folds of skin around head

Very long ears

Short legs

Huge feet

Beagle

Beagles are always ready for action. They love being part of a family, or a pack. Look out for their wagging tails when they are doing something fun.

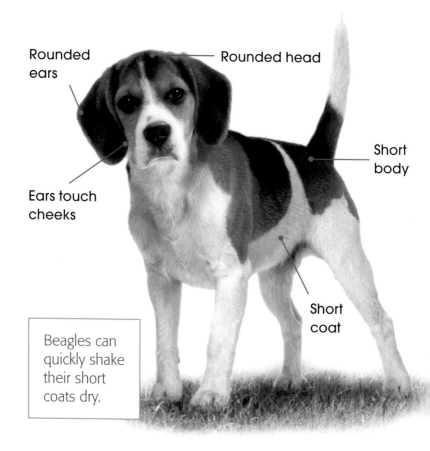

Rounded ears

Rounded head

Ears touch cheeks

Short body

Short coat

Beagles can quickly shake their short coats dry.

Border Collie

Look out for Border Collies on farms. They love to work hard. They make good sheepdogs. Border Collies learn quickly. When the farmer makes a special sound or action, they know what to do.

Border Collies have been trained as mountain rescue dogs. They can find people who are lost or hurt.

Brown eyes

Black and white coat

Border Terrier

Border Terriers are action dogs that love rough-and-tumble games. Long legs make them as speedy as bigger dogs.

The first Border Terriers came from the area between England and Scotland.

Small, folded ears

Short tail

Short muzzle

Thick, rough coat

Long legs

Boxer

Boxers are brave and make good guard dogs. They are popular pets too. Boxers love to play and have fun. Just watch out for the drool!

Short, square head

Short nose

White markings

Boxers are very loyal dogs. They love and protect their owners.

Short, shiny coat

Brown or tawny fur

This boxer has a brindle coat, with streaks of different colours.

Bulldog

Bulldogs have grumpy-looking faces but they are actually friendly, happy dogs. Bulldogs get tired quickly, so they like slow, short walks.

Some Bulldogs have bad habits, like snoring and drooling!

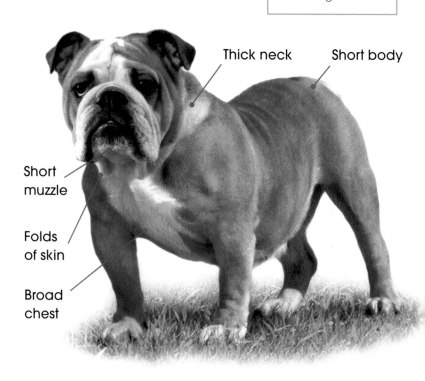

Thick neck

Short body

Short muzzle

Folds of skin

Broad chest

The Bulldog is the national dog of Great Britain.

Cavalier King Charles Spaniel

These sweet dogs were popular palace pets 400 years ago. They are famous for their sad-looking eyes, but they are happy dogs that love to play!

The long fur on this dog's ears and tail needs plenty of brushing to keep it free from tangles.

Large, dark eyes

Very long, hairy ears

Long, silky coat

Feathered tail

Short, square muzzle

King Charles Spaniels look similar, but they are smaller.

Chihuahua

These are the smallest dogs in the world. Chihuahuas are popular pets in towns and cities, because they do not need much exercise.

Chihuahuas are named after a state in Mexico.

Chihuahuas are part of a group of dogs known as 'toy' dogs.

Large, round eyes

Large ears

Tail curls over back

Ruff

Tiny body

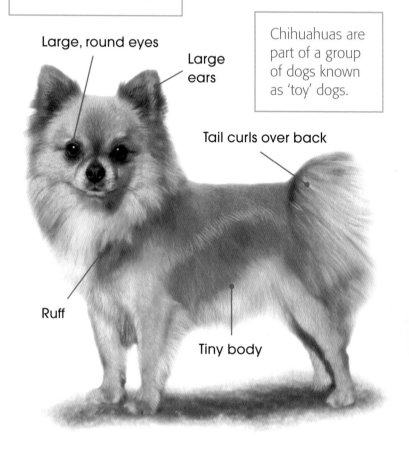

Cocker Spaniel

Busy, bouncy Cocker Spaniels love going on walks. Spot them sniffing around and carrying objects in their mouths.

American Cocker Spaniels are smaller than English Cocker Spaniels. Look out for them at dog shows.

Floppy ears with long hair

Square muzzle

Long, silky coat

American Cocker Spaniel

English Cocker Spaniel

Dachshund

Long bodies and short legs give Dachshunds their 'sausage dog' nickname. Dachshunds may be tiny, but they have a loud bark and make great watchdogs.

Dachshunds can have smooth hair, long hair, or wiry hair.

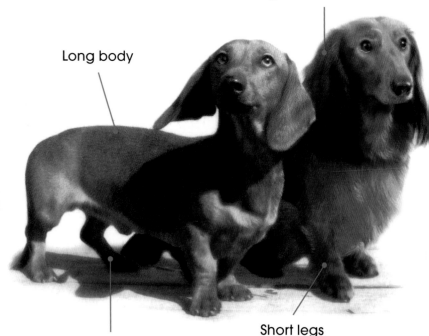

Long-haired Dachshund

Long body

Smooth-haired Dachshund

Short legs

Dalmatian

Dalmatian puppies are born with plain white coats. Their spots appear after two or three weeks. Dalmatians have lots of energy and love to run.

Dalmatians used to be called 'firehouse dogs'. They were bred to run along next to horse-drawn carriages, including old-fashioned fire engines!

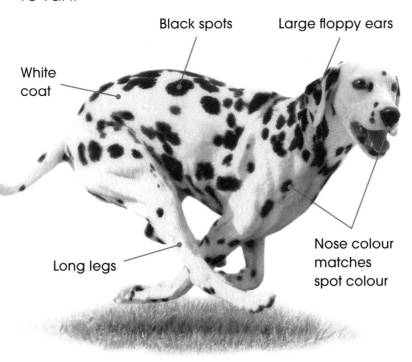

Black spots

Large floppy ears

White coat

Nose colour matches spot colour

Long legs

English Springer Spaniel

Springer Spaniels are cheerful and cheeky. Spot their tails wagging as these friendly dogs come to say hello.

Some Springer Spaniels work as gundogs.

Long, flat ears

Long, soft coat

Feathered fur on legs, ears, and belly

German Shepherd Dog

German Shepherd Dogs are working dogs. They were bred to herd sheep but can be trained as guide dogs, police dogs, and guard dogs. They are popular pets too.

German Shepherd Dogs are also known as 'Alsatians'.

Long body

Brown eyes

Long muzzle

Long, bushy tail

Thick, woolly fur

Strong legs

Golden Retriever

Golden Retrievers are very popular pets. You can also spot them working as gundogs, police dogs, and guide dogs. They are friendly, gentle, and easy to train.

Broad head

Dark-brown eyes

Cream or golden coat

Wide muzzle

Wavy fur

Long tails help Golden Retrievers to steer when they swim.

Great Dane

Great Danes are huge but gentle. Like other large breeds they need plenty of space and plenty of food.

Great Danes are the national dogs of Germany.

Round eyes

Triangle-shaped ears

Long legs

Short, glossy coat

Irish Wolfhound

Gigantic Irish Wolfhounds are the world's tallest dogs. They are friendly pets.

Seven huge Wolfhounds were once sent to Ancient Rome as a gift. The Romans were amazed.

Small ears

Shaggy coat

Long head and muzzle

Labrador Retriever

Large, bouncy Labradors are some of the world's most popular dogs. They were bred to fetch things for people, so they love playing and long walks.

Labradors love swimming and splashing in water. Their thick coats keep them dry and warm.

Brown or hazel eyes

Strong neck

Short, thick coat

Thick tail covered in short fur

Look out for Labradors with yellow, black, or chocolate coats.

Newfoundland

These large dogs are popular family pets. Newfoundlands love having fun with children. They also like to swim, and are strong enough to pull a rowing boat.

A Newfoundland called Nana stars in the famous story *Peter Pan*.

Large head

Dark coat

Small brown eyes

Thick fur

Newfoundlands are good at rescuing people who get into trouble in water.

Old English Sheepdog

A thick, shaggy coat makes these dogs look like woolly sheep. They are actually named after the sheep-herding work they were bred to do.

Old English Sheepdogs are good family pets, because they like to protect children they love.

Fur covers eyes

Small ears

Grey or blue fur

White head, neck, front legs, and belly

Shaggy coat

Parson Jack Russell Terrier

Jack Russells are named after the first person to breed them. They are brave dogs with lots of energy. If they get bored, Jack Russells can get up to lots of mischief!

V-shaped folded ears

Straight tail

Straight back

Look out for Jack Russells with smooth and rough coats.

Pointer

These gundogs can hear and smell much better than people. They can show their owners where a smell is coming from by pointing with their noses.

Look out for Pointers walking with their nose to the ground. They like following scents.

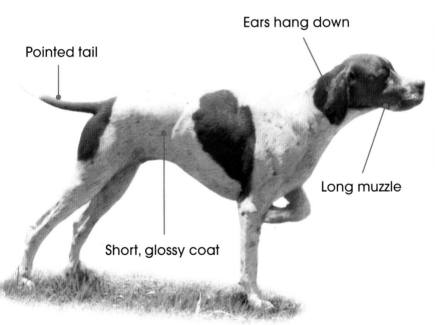

Ears hang down

Pointed tail

Long muzzle

Short, glossy coat

Pomeranian

A Pomeranian's face is almost hidden by the long, thick fur around its neck and shoulders. Listen out for these toy dogs barking loudly when they see or hear something new.

Tail curls over back

Fox-like face

Very fluffy coat

Queen Victoria kept pet Pomeranians.

Poodle

Poodles like to be groomed. Their fur can be trimmed into fancy shapes and patterns. They are clever dogs that love learning new tricks.

There are three different types of poodle to spot – Standard, Toy, and Miniature.

Standard Poodle

Long ears

Poodles are utility dogs.

Large body

Thick, long coat

Long legs

Toy Poodle

Small body

 # Pug

Pugs have been popular pets for hundreds of years. Large eyes and 'squashed' faces make these toy dogs look super cute.

Pugs look like tiny versions of a huge working dog called a Mastiff.

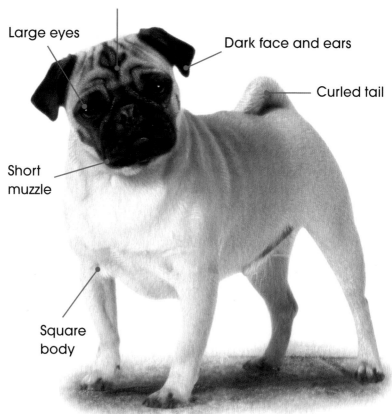

Wrinkled skin

Large eyes

Dark face and ears

Curled tail

Short muzzle

Square body

Rough Collie

Rough Collies are famous for their huge manes of thick fur. They are sweet and friendly dogs that will do anything to protect their family.

A Rough Collie's fur needs grooming to keep it looking beautiful.

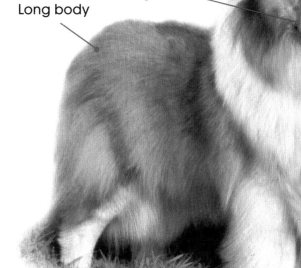

Long body

Long muzzle

Thick coat

Not all Collies have long coats. Look out for Smooth Collies too.

Schnauzer

The first Schnauzers were clever, hard-working farm dogs. Today there are three types to spot. Miniature Schnauzers are the most popular.

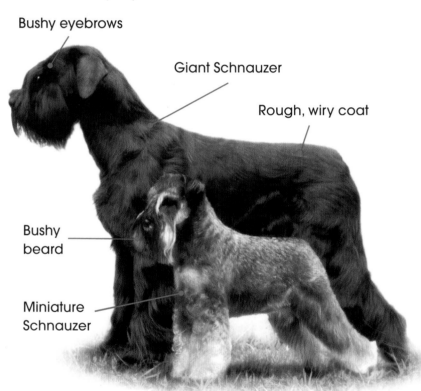

Bushy eyebrows

Giant Schnauzer

Rough, wiry coat

Bushy beard

Miniature Schnauzer

This Miniature Schnauzer has a salt-and-pepper coat.

Scottish Terrier

'Scottie' dogs can be black, pale cream, or brindle – a mixture of two colours. Watch out for Scotties zooming across the ground as they play.

Pointed ears

Bushy eyebrows

Long head

Wiry fur

Short legs

Shih Tzu

Shih Tzu means 'lion dog'. These utility dogs are as brave as lions, but friendly not fierce. If you spot one, look at the hair over its nose – it grows straight up!

Tail curled over back

Large ears

Beard

Long coat

Don't get the Shih Tzu mixed up with the Lhasa Apso. The breeds look similar.

Siberian Husky

The first Siberian Huskies came from the cold Arctic. These dogs love working in teams to pull sleds over ice and snow.

Huskies are brilliant at jumping and digging. They are hard to keep as pets because they easily escape.

Each eye can be more than one colour

Fluffy tail

Webbed feet with fur between the toes

 # St Bernard

St Bernards became famous for being mountain rescue dogs. They are strong enough to pull people on a sled. Large furry feet help them to pad through snow.

St Bernards make friendly pets. Owners need a big house and garden, and plenty of dog food!

Ears close to cheeks

Huge body and head

Long tail

Welsh Corgi

There are two breeds of Welsh Corgi, called Cardigan and Pembroke. They like busy days, good meals, and muddy walks.

Pembroke Corgis have lived in Buckingham Palace, London, for many years. They are Queen Elizabeth II's favourite dogs.

Fox-like head shape

Medium-sized ears

Pembroke Corgi

Short legs

Corgis are pastoral dogs. They were bred to herd cattle.

West Highland White Terrier

Pure white fur and cheeky faces make 'Westies' easy to spot. These small dogs are full of energy and ready to have fun.

West Highland White Terriers have rough coats that need plenty of brushing.

Straight tail

Black nose

White coat

Small body

Short, strong legs

Whippet

Whippets were bred
to run very fast. Some
Whippets take part in
races on special tracks.

Look out for
Whippets wearing
jackets to keep
them warm in
cold weather.

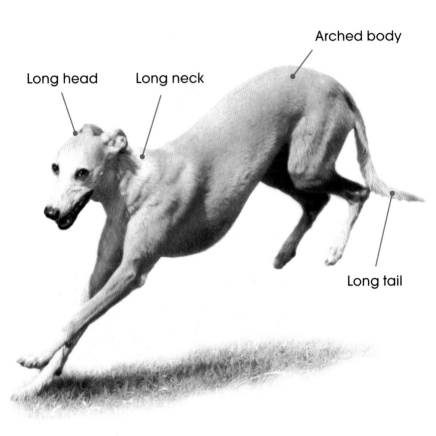

Arched body

Long head   Long neck

Long tail

Yorkshire Terrier

Yorkshire Terriers are tiny but tough. They look pretty at dog shows, but love to run around and get messy in the park. Spot them making friends with much bigger dogs.

A bow keeps the Yorkshire Terrier's long hair out of its eyes.

Small ears

Black nose

Tan hair

Steel-blue hair

Long, shiny coat

Listen out for noisy Yorkshire Terrier barks.

Breed groups

 Gundogs were bred to help people find or fetch game animals.

 Hounds were bred to find animals, using their excellent eyes or noses.

 Working dogs were bred to help people do jobs, from search and rescue to guarding.

 Pastoral dogs were bred to do farm jobs, such as herding cows and sheep.

 Terriers were bred to get into small spaces.

 Toy dogs were bred to keep people company.

 Utility dogs were bred to carry out many different tasks.

Spotter's guide

How many of these dogs have
you seen? Tick them when you
spot them.

☐ Afghan Hound
page 6

☐ Basset Hound
page 7

☐ Beagle
page 8

☐ Border Collie
page 9

☐ Border Terrier
page 10

☐ Boxer
page 11

☐ **Bulldog**
page 12

☐ **Cavalier King Charles Spaniel**
page 13

☐ **Chihuahua**
page 14

☐ **Cocker Spaniel**
page 15

☐ **Dachshund**
page 16

☐ **Dalmatian**
page 17

☐ **English Springer Spaniel**
page 18

☐ **German Shepherd Dog**
page 19

43

Golden Retriever
page 20

Great Dane
page 21

Irish Wolfhound
page 22

Labrador Retriever
page 23

Newfoundland
page 24

Old English Sheepdog
page 25

Parson Jack Russell Terrier
page 26

Pointer
page 27

44

Pomeranian
page 28

Poodle
page 29

Pug
page 30

Rough Collie
page 31

Schnauzer
page 32

Scottish Terrier
page 33

Shih Tzu
page 34

Siberian Husky
page 35

St Bernard
page 36

Welsh Corgi
page 37

West Highland
White Terrier
page 38

Whippet
page 39

Yorkshire Terrier
page 40

Useful words

bred reared to look or behave in a certain way

breed a type of dog

brindle brown or tawny-coloured fur with streaks of different colours

coat the fur that covers a dog

drool the spit that leaks from the mouth of some types of dogs

feathered long and fluffy

groom to brush and clean a dog's coat

scent smell

Find out more

If you would like to find out more about dogs, start with these websites. You will discover where to visit a dog show, and how to care for pet dogs.

The Young Kennel Club
www.ykc.org.uk

Crufts – The World's Largest Dog Show
www.crufts.org.uk

The Kennel Club's guide to keeping safe around dogs
www.thekennelclub.org.uk/safeandsound